Egg Shaped Ball

by Laura DiNovis Berry

INDIES UNITED PUBLISHING HOUSE, LLC

Copyright © by Laura DiNovis Berry

First Edition published March 2020
Published by Indies United Publishing House, LLC

Cover art designed by YaYa Designs

All rights reserved worldwide. No part of this publication may be replicated, redistributed, or given away in any form without the prior written consent of the author/publisher or the terms relayed to you herein.

ISBN-13: 978-1-64456-101-0
Library of Congress Control Number: 2020931310

INDIES UNITED PUBLISHING HOUSE, LLC
P.O. BOX 3071
QUINCY, IL 62305-3071
www.indiesunited.net

Dedication

This chapbook is dedicated to every player
who has ever gotten the side eye and incredulous,
"You play rugby?"

Yes. We do.

As a big rugby fan, I loved the Egged Shaped Ball. The poems fitted nicely with the various aspects of the game and delivered punchy messages.

~ Brian Groves, poet

Berry's collection of poems reminds me a little bit of Kwame Alexander's The Crossover. What Kwame Alexander does with basketball as a metaphor for life and battling racism, so does Berry seem to be doing with rugby. There appears to be a nod toward some feminist themes related to women learning to be quick and wily in what is otherwise a "man's world." Also present throughout the collect is the idea of breaking loose from the way society defines what a woman is supposed to be.

The poetic structure is free verse. Berry employs sound devices like alliteration, onomatopoeia, and repetition to capture the experience of playing rugby. She also uses animal and earth imagery throughout the work. This, too, helps to capture the spirit of rugby.

Overall, her work is multi-layered, well-written, well-arranged, and contains clear thematic development throughout the collection.

~Timothy Baldwin, author

The poet was clever, very visual and touched some nerves!

~JuliaPicks1, Book Reviewer

Table of Contents

Meet the Players - 3
Failed Tackle - 7
Always a Sub, Never a Start - 9
Comet - 11
Post Game Revelry - 13
Running With White Horses - 15
Snowglobe - 17
First Contact - 19
A Rugby Player Scoffs At Victim Blaming
After Being Tackled Repeatedly
By The Men On Her Team - 21
The Breakaway - 25
Bruises Are Medals - 27
A.R. (After Rugby) - 29
Snowstorm on the Pitch - 31
Egg Shaped Ball - 33

EGG SHAPED BALL

PLAY LIKE A GIRL

LAURA DiNOVIS BERRY

Meet the Players:

I. Forwards

2) Hooker: Crafty and nimble, a thief in their midst- her leg a lockpick

1) Loose Head Prop: Aims to crush with her diamond shoulders and will of iron

3) Tight Head Prop: She grinds the world to dust with legs and legs of iron

4) Locks: Gripped together, (5)they propel the group forward - a battering ram

6) Blindside Flanker: She's prepped for a hard explosion- A patient missile

7) Open Flanker: Wolf seeking prey, she waits for the perfect time to strike

8) Eight: She is stalwart, gaining yardage crash by crash - never giving up

LAURA DiNOVIS BERRY

II. Backs

9) Scrum-half: She is a link between the two worlds of brute power and speed

10) Fly-half: A captain strategizing, commanding these players' movements

12) Insider Center: Less woman, more wild horse. She tramples, charges, bucks

13) Outside Center: She complements her counterpart - ready to run, fight

11) Left Wing: is jealous of this woman; she's faster than light

14) Right Wing: She is like a bolt shot from a crossbow, an uncatchable foe

15) Full Back: A piece of the spine, she thinks like a shark - with laser focus

LAURA DiNOVIS BERRY

Failed Tackle

Ready now. Steady.

Watch the hips - not their eyes!

Unlock your muscles. SNAP as cobras do.

Grit teeth to plastic. Fingers slip over fabric.

Dirt in your grasp instead of flesh.

Break into panic.

Despair.

Breathe, breathe, recover.

Yes, you will rush again.

You must.

Always a Sub, Never a Starter

Glazed green eyes track the starting players.

Metaphorical glass between desired spaces and benched reality becomes smudged with grubby fingerprints.

Hot, jealous breath steams off those backs with bold white numbers.

So many injurious hexes are cast after them,

one by one…

LAURA DiNOVIS BERRY

Comet

The lingering trail of fire is mesmerizing.

How can you look away from her?

A comet scorching earth,

destroying every body in her trajectory.

She combusts at her destination,

appearing as a constellation of triumphant stars.

LAURA DiNOVIS BERRY

NOTES & QUESTIONS

Post Game Revelry

The fairer sex may be female, but
>don't think we hide from a good keg of beer or from
>shooting that boot!

Foes and friends both sing in lusty
>voices - recount the awesome feats of strength displayed on
>the perfect

pitch. Hard hits are praised, try's flaunted.
>Beers are chugged to hail the best rugger from each team.
>This drink up heals

bones and hurt pride, as well as
>bonds these two opposing groups. These women need each
>other to prove doubters

wrong, to show that rugby is not
>just for men. "Tackle her!" they'll scream on the pitch
>just try and stop them.

Running with White Horses
-Dedicated to the Phoenixville White Horse Women's Rugby Club

Imagined to be gentle, serene -
the ensuing stampede is always unexpected.

Hooves crush bodies, score the earth.
Their onslaught is the epicenter of tremor after tremor.

Thunder bellows from the ground.
The sky is a silent witness;
the White Horses have wracked ruin again.

Snowglobe

A snowglobe,
each flake a thought,
sits atop her shoulders.
She's emboldened,
launching herself forward with youthful fury.
But the technique's wrong,
the globe is sent into a snowstorm.
Its contents float as if gravity has evaporated.
But she gives a plucky twirl to hide the damage,
twisting so no cracks are visible.
The snowstorm whirls on and on,
unseen.
It is late when the team bus' vibrations shake her.
Broken glass scatters,
an avalanche of nausea rolls over her.
She is prone forever,
collecting all the shards.

LAURA DiNOVIS BERRY

First Contact

Ears roar blood
before first contact

Shoulder breaks into
spongy flesh above the hip

Hands reaching around the knees
grasping for each other
as drowning swimmers do
ready to squeeze out the life of their rescuer

Crashing down into oblivion

NOTES & QUESTIONS

A Rugby Player Scoffs At Victim Blaming After Being Tackled Repeatedly By The Men On Her Team

They're bigger up close.
Stronger than you'd think too.
Snorting bulls and agile lynxes,
all chasing and tackling whoever holds the ball.
After being crushed by friendly brothers in play,
I must laugh at the question,
"Why didn't you fight back?"

Come here. Come see.
Try your luck wriggling out
from under two hundred pounds
of determination, of rage, of solid want.

It's true, we can serve cold punishment too.
A hard shoulder drive, some nice footwork,
but we must be clever, quick -
wily.

Once caught, escape is rare.

So come. Come be crushed!

EGG SHAPED BALL

Tryrunningwiththewindpunchedfromyou,
after
        blows
to
  the
     head
leave
       you
spinning.

As the muscles in your body scream...
THEN.

Then you may ask your questions.

The Breakaway

Racing
across the field
shattering air.

Legs scramble
from yards away,
desperate to intercept.

LAURA DiNOVIS BERRY

Bruises Are Medals

Masochists:
Bruises are medals and badges we flaunt.
    Our flesh is stretched before everyone, anyone.
We prance as Lipizzans, showcasing every limp.
    Thighs display gouges and thumbprints.
Courtesans coquettishly giggling,
    "Look at what could not stop us."

Sadists:
Our hearts are full of sneers.
    The scrum of flesh becomes a battering ram.
Humans once, now a pack of Minotaurs.
    Hindquarters carving ravines, eager to churn through the fallen.
Our cadence is a call for a massacre.
    "Crush them, Crush them, Crush them"

A.R.
(After Rugby)

There was a blank before rugby,
but when she played she felt so free...
Once stuck, she could now flourish - grow
into animal or rainbow.
        She touched that ball and felt lucky.

Lucky to run, become bloody
and stand with a smile - all muddy.
She developed confidence so
        she kept learning and thriving..

She found team politics funny,
but even if fights got ugly
her team was always there to show
support for their community.
Her home is buggy but sturdy.
        She keeps learning and thriving...

Snowstorm on the Pitch

Biting.
Pounding.
Numbing.
Chilling.
The pain of the biting, pounding fray
magnified on a numbing, chilling day.

Egg Shaped Ball

You would been have seething before. Back in the days when you'd first gotten your hands on that egg shaped ball and felt something click into place with a snarl. Fighting for the privilege to be smeared to shit on a dirty field meant everything. The 'tick, tick' of a stopwatch matched the ticking of the veins below your eyes because coach didn't put you in and those cliquey bitches who whined and tackled and sniffled and hit their way to starter were taking your time. Your time. Now you stand whooping and shouting with your blood up so happy, so fucking happy to be alive - to be here - to be covered in dirt and bruises and older and slower and so happy to touch that egg every once in awhile. You are so happy now.

About The Poet

After having once been forced by circumstance to ignore poetry, Laura DiNovis Berry has since dedicated her life to it. She has fallen madly, deeply in love with this craft.

In addition to writing poetry, Berry also provides free reviews at Berry's Poetry Book Reviews for her fellow poets in hopes that modern poetry can be shared with a wider audience.

Curious about rugby? Curious about anything at all in this text? Feel free to contact Berry on Twitter at @maudlinkahn or at BerrysBooks.com

www.ingramcontent.com/pod-product-compliance
Lightning Source LLC
Chambersburg PA
CBHW070121110526
44587CB00018BA/3336

These poems race down the pitch and each syllable pumps ferociously happy blood. Dedicated to rugby and the women who play it, this chapbook honors the intense lows and electric highs a player can feel when she laces up her cleats.

INDIES UNITED
PUBLISHING HOUSE, LLC